Global Leadership Ltd UK

The

NUCLEAR WAR

Game

Transforming Global Security

Gordan Glass

www.GlobalLeadershipLtd.com

The Small Print

In providing this content, the author is acting in the manner and role of an investigative journalist and whistleblower, in that he is bringing information and alternative viewpoints into public awareness with the intention of increasing the range of understanding of the reader in the wider public interest.

The author believes the content to be true, but makes no warranty, claim, proposition or suggestion that it is: it is presented as the author's personal opinion only and readers are asked to judge for themselves the limits of their own agreement with the content and to recognize their conclusions as their own subjective judgments. Neither the publisher nor the author shall be held liable for any errors, offence, harm, loss or any other damages, however caused, resulting from the use of this report or its contents: caveat lector.

Furthermore, the information provided within must not be relied upon as being up to date and must not be relied upon as legal or professional advice, nor as a substitute for such, as different professionals may have different opinions on the content.

All links provided are for information and reference only and no warranty is provided or implied regarding the content or accuracy of any related material.

DEDICATION

This book is dedicated to the work of Wilton Park, in its endeavours to resolve some of the most difficult and pressing problems in international affairs, by providing a caring and supportive discussion environment along with truly outstanding service and facilities. It is always a pleasure and an honour to attend a meeting at Wilton Park.

Table of Contents

"since wars begin in the minds of men, it is in the minds of men that the defences of peace must be constructed"

- First line of the UNESCO Constitution, 1945

Section 1:

Introduction

Chapter 1:

A conference & a movie

A conference

The purpose of this book is to provide a report on a conference, which the author attended in December 2014, relating to the Nuclear Weapons Non-Proliferation Treaty and to provide a series of observations about how the issue of nuclear disarmament – and disarmament generally – can be moved forward.

This book will cover the following topics:

- The author's understanding of his role as facilitator in this process.

- His view of the hypocrisy that is endemic in the Non-

Proliferation Treaty and the issue of disarmament.

- A description of a model of transformation and paradigm shift – through which two concurrent but opposing truths can be resolved into a higher level of understanding.

- The problem of lack of trust and how to rebuild it.

- A new vision of the way forward.

This report does not endeavour to be an academic work: it was dictated within one day. It is designed to be an easily consumed overview, which provides unusual perspectives and understandings brought in from other disciplines and experiences.

The overall objective is to resolve the current differences in perspective in the territory of disarmament and to hasten the disarmament process, in accordance with what appear to be the wishes of the majority of the public throughout the world.

A movie

The title of this book is based upon "The War Game", the title of a highly provocative movie, produced in 1965, about the inconsistencies in UK Government public policy and inability to deal with the practical aftermath of even a very limited nuclear attack. The movie was produced and directed by Peter Watkins for the BBC but then banned – also by the BBC Board, under pressure from the Government – for 20 years from TV screens worldwide.

This movie had a profound effect upon the author at the time, when he saw it in a restricted cinema release, and its legacy lives on. This book is being published on the 50th anniversary of this movie. The reality is that what was shown in that movie still prevails – only far worse: life on the planet could still be destroyed by one accidental incident of nuclear war by the many thousands of weapons on permanent instant alert.

The NUCLEAR WAR Game

Chapter 2:

The author's role

In December 2014, the author attended a conference at the UK Foreign Office Conference Centre at Wilton Park on the subject of the nuclear Non-Proliferation Treaty. This was the UK pre-meeting for the United Nations Review Conference relating to the Non-Proliferation Treaty (NPT) to be held in New York in April 2015. This UN Review Conference has been a five yearly activity since the Non-Proliferation Treaty was opened for signature in 1968 and came into force in 1970.

The author has a history of association with this topic; having ancestors from different parts of the world he felt, from early childhood, that he was born a global citizen, transcending the artificial geographical limitations of nation states. As well as being a UK citizen he was brought up to support the principles of the United Nations – especially the desire to "end the scourge of war" – in particular because his mother's family (German) and father's family (British) were from opposite sides of the Second World War. His childhood was coloured by stories about the Second World War and its consequences at family level.

A teenager's view of the nuclear issue

He was a teenager in the 1960s when the threat of nuclear weapons was so great and palpable that it seemed that one person could destroy all human life on the planet at the press of a button. In the late 1960s he travelled to New York to see the then UN Secretary General, U Thant, to express his strong view that something needed to change in this situation. That was just before the Non-Proliferation Treaty came into force. That treaty was a great relief for the world, seeming to be a clear step towards a solution.

The author returned to this field in 2004, when he attended the very same Wilton Park UN pre-meeting conference 10 years ago. This was just after the Iraq War and the subsequent UN Conference in 2005 was considered a failure. The author felt the Wilton Park Conference in 2004 was an illustration of how the governments could not be relied upon to make any important decision in the world; he left that conference determined to work towards setting up a project for a global parliament as an alternative way of making global decisions in accordance with the wishes of the people.

A UN Parliamentary Assembly

That project turned into the NGO Campaign for a UN Parliamentary Assembly (unpacampaign.org), which is a project to give a voice for the people of the world within the UN decision-making process. This is a real global project, which has gained, and continues to gain, substantial cross-party support from parliamentarians, government ministers, NGOs and activists around the world.

The Wilton Park Conference was attended mainly by ambassadors and participants with Government positions, so most of the people there were being paid to take certain views and certain positions. The conference was held under Chatham House Rules.

The value of a neutral party

The author, as a self-funded neutral party, saw his role as a facilitator, representing the possibility of a resolution of the differences between the two sides, enabling the creation of a transformed state to bring about the reality of global disarmament. He saw his role was to work directly towards the resolution of the differences that were palpable at the conference.

Having attended the Wilton Park pre-meetings in 2004, 2009 and 2014, his observation is that there has been a very significant change in the feeling within those conferences. In 2004 there was a great feeling of angst and fear; in 2009 there was a feeling of optimism after a speech President Obama had given in Prague and in 2014 there was a sense of both frustration and resignation at the lack of progress after the 2010 conference – that conference had resulted in a 64 point action plan, but very few of those points had been followed through. For the author this provided a point of optimism as an opportunity to move beyond the differences. Frustration can be a powerful motivator for change. Yet that possibility and potential did not seem to be clear to the majority of parties at the conference.

The NUCLEAR WAR Game

Section 2:

The Non-Proliferation Treaty

Chapter 3:

Background of the NPT

It is worth outlining here the background for the Non-Proliferation Treaty (NPT) to give a context for what follows. This report relates specifically to the obligation the Nation States have under Article VI of the Treaty to work for disarmament. This report does not deal with the other aspects of the treaty, particularly those relating to control of fissile materials where progress is being made.

Article VI of the NPT says that: "Each of the parties to the Treaty undertakes to pursue negotiations in good faith on effective measures relating to cessation of the nuclear arms race at an early date and to nuclear disarmament, and on a treaty on general and complete disarmament under strict and effective international control."

Little progress made

The central problem relating to this Treaty is that despite the pressure of the non-nuclear weapon states (NNWS), the nuclear weapon states (NWS) have not made very much progress in terms of the cessation of the nuclear arms race and nuclear disarmament.

The basis of the Treaty is, on one hand, in Article I, the declaration that certain nation states had nuclear weapons. In 1967, there were five nations that did have them: USA, Russia, China, France and the UK. Those are the nuclear weapon states (NWS) Parties to the Treaty – a tiny subset of the 187 states in total who are Parties to it.

The other hand of the Treaty, was that the NNWS could have access (under Article IV) to "equipment, materials and scientific and technological information" for the "development of the applications of nuclear energy for peaceful uses" only, such as the generation of electricity, and that (under Article II) they would "not manufacture or otherwise acquire nuclear weapons or other nuclear explosive devices".

The states that did not sign

A major problem with the Treaty, however, is that some states did not sign it: for example Israel, Pakistan and India, who all went on to develop nuclear weapons. North Korea left the Treaty and also developed nuclear weapons and Iran appears to be operating at the boundaries of possibility as to what it is allowed to do under the Treaty, although it remains a signatory of the Treaty and a member of the NNWS.

No end date

The Treaty came into force in 1970 and was to last 25 years. At the end of those 25 years, in 1995, the NWS proposed that the Treaty should be extended indefinitely. This was agreed and, importantly, leaves the NWS with a commitment and an obligation to disarm but with no end date for doing so.

The NWS, on their part, say that they have reduced their arsenals considerably, but there are still many thousands of nuclear weapons that are deployed in various countries ready for immediate launch.

To summarise, in relation to Article VI (the disarmament chapter) of the NPT, NNWS continue to put pressure on NWS to achieve total nuclear disarmament. In fact there are many states that want to move to complete disarmament, not just nuclear disarmament.

Disarmament is built into the UN Charter

The concept of disarmament was built into the United Nations Charter, which was signed in 1945. It is important to note that Article 11 of the UN Charter authorised the General Assembly to consider "the principles governing disarmament and the regulation of armaments". A major objective of the UN was, and remains, "the maintenance of international peace and security" in the world and particularly, according to the Charter Preamble, "to save succeeding generations from the scourge of war". The scourge of war was very clearly in the minds of the parties who signed the UN Charter after the devastating effect of the two world wars; the Second World War had just ended when the UN Charter was signed in 1945.

The very first resolution adopted by the UN General Assembly in 1946 called for "the elimination from national armaments of atomic weapons and of all other major weapons adaptable to mass destruction".

UN General Assembly's work on disarmament is supposedly to be conducted through the independent Conference on Disarmament. In relation to disarmament, however, this Conference has failed to achieve much significant progress in over 50 years since it started as the Disarmament Committee in 1962, apart from the Comprehensive Test Ban Treaty in 1996.

The issue needs to be resolved

The issue of disarmament has therefore been long-running and has been a primary source of insecurity in the world for the last 70 years. Nuclear weapons represent the greatest source of power in the world, the greatest potential for destruction of human life and the greatest threat to peace and security in the world. It is therefore the key issue that needs to be resolved in order to de-escalate threats and violence around the world. In other words, if the nuclear weapons standoff has not been resolved, there is little hope for movement towards disarmament with non-nuclear weapons.

Chapter 4:

The UN Security Council

One of the key problems in relation to the NPT is that the five nuclear weapon powers (the N5) within the NPT are also the five permanent members (the P5) that have the veto over decisions on the UN Security Council, which is the UN body responsible for peace and security in the world; and yet those five powers, as well as having nuclear weapons, are also the principal manufacturers of weapons in the world and the principal distributors of weapons to other countries and to private individuals. It can be noted that, far from maintaining peace and security, those five nations are responsible for the complete opposite: maintaining threats and violence in the world. Indeed the UN Security Council has come to be seen as a place to authorise war rather than maintain peace.

The NUCLEAR WAR Game

There have been many attempts to reform the basic inadequacies of the UN Security Council but these have, in practice, achieved little. The principle inadequacies are:

1. The UNSC decision-making is run by the five P5 states, with veto powers, out of almost 200 member states of the UNGA.

2. The UNGA delegates decision-making relating to peace and security to the UNSC.

3. The UNSC is assuming the role of global lawmaker, but with no real democratic legitimacy, and in particular is not representative of the diversity of global values or global public opinion.

4. The P5 are the major nuclear weapon powers.

5. The P5 are the principle arms and weapons manufacturers and distributors in the world, which directly conflicts with their UN duty to maintain peace and security.

6. The problem at the heart of the UN is that the P5 maintain the emphasis on a limited perception of

military and economic threats and military solutions as the primary way of dealing with breaches of the peace and differences of opinions, both within and between member states.

The UNSC is the therefore the major area of dysfunction within the UN and is most responsible for the UN being seen as incapable of maintaining peace and security in the world: the P5 are still trying to run the world on the far outdated basis that they won World War II, 70 years ago, with nuclear weapons.

Moreover, the UNSC and the P5 are incapable of doing anything about the other (N4) nuclear powers, which are left isolated outside both the UNSC and the NPT.

The NUCLEAR WAR Game

Chapter 5:

The problem of nuclear weapons

It is worth highlighting at this point what the problems with nuclear weapons are:

- **Humanitarian consequences**

By far the most significant fact is that nuclear weapons have the ability to destroy all human life on this planet in one incident. In fact there are so many nuclear weapons in existence that all human life could be destroyed many times over. The power to do this effectively rests in the hands of any one of the leaders of the nation states who have nuclear weapons. Any one of them could initiate this process. This could also happen automatically: the Russians, at least, are understood to have a system designed to launch nuclear weapons automatically under certain situations, without human intervention.

The Humanitarian Statement on nuclear weapons signed by 124 UN member states and delivered to the UN First Committee in October 2013 by New Zealand said: "no state or international body could address the immediate humanitarian emergency caused by a nuclear weapon detonation or provide adequate assistance to victims".

- **Risks of accidents**

There have been a number of occurrences where nuclear weapons have almost been launched inadvertently. The author remembers Mikhail Gorbachev being asked how close Russia and America came to nuclear war. Gorbachev took a deep breath and said, "Very close". It was in that deep breath that one could sense how close it was. Indeed, even in the late '90s there was reportedly an incident where President Yeltsin was obliged to press the button, which had been placed on his desk, to launch Russia's nuclear weapons, but decided not to. All the protocols said he should have done it, but thankfully, he did not do so. There have been a number of documented instances like this and the risks continue.

Some sources say the risk of accident is very high. Indeed, the very nature and secrecy surrounding nuclear weapons means that no good risk assessment can be made about what is, after all, probably the greatest risk to human life on our planet.

- **Expense**

Most NWS have to spend an extraordinary amount of money maintaining their arsenal on full alert in the hope that it will never be used. Maintaining a system with the intention of never using it can be seen as a total waste of money.

The weapons go out of date, and the states which have them believe that they need to replace them; they also need to destroy the old ones. Many of the arrangements to get rid of nuclear weapons in the name of disarmament have in fact been a simple matter of destroying outdated weapons. Yet destruction of nuclear materials is not easy or cheap. Hence the USA reportedly disposed of depleted uranium in bombs dropped upon Iraq.

- **Issue of Control**

The presidents of the countries involved supposedly have effective individual ability to authorise the launch of a nuclear strike. This system, however, is not one that is under democratic control. The timeframe for decision-making is too short to debate the matter in parliament and to obtain the views or consensus of the people. Moreover, there is no possibility of ascertaining the views of the government, or the people, of the target state. At best, therefore, any decision to launch relies haphazardly on the frame of mind of one person at any one moment. There are also some reports that even this system can be bypassed by the military in some NWS if they wish to do so.

This adds to the uncertainties of risk, and also illustrates that even in supposedly democratic countries the matter is not under democratic control.

- **Morality and legality of weapons**

Over the last 70 years, since the bombing of Hiroshima

and Nagasaki by the United States, the understandings related to morality and legality have moved on considerably. Nuclear weapons have been described as the greatest evil on the planet, so it is something of a paradox that the NWS justify their existence in the name of defending themselves against the perceived evil of an attack, fighting perceived evil with yet more evil. Elsewhere, the author has shown that the perception of evil is an illusion in the mind of the beholder.

The legality was brought into question very forcibly by the International Court of Justice, where the Court made a number of rulings not only against the legality of the use of nuclear weapons but also regarding the legality of the threat of using them. These decisions were only advisory opinions of the Court but are the best statement on legality under international law that has been made to date.

- **The renewal and modernisation process**

As weapons become outdated they need to be renewed and this renewal process conflicts directly with the commitment to disarmament. If the nuclear weapons states are committed to disarmament "in good faith" how can they justify developing them and renewing them, modernising the system? There is a basic inconsistency and hypocrisy in this process.

- **Hypocrisy**

As can be seen from what has been stated so far, the central issue relating to NWS and the maintenance of nuclear weapons is one of hypocrisy, where the NWS have signed the NPT to get rid of them and yet maintain them, develop them, and renew them.

- **The illusory belief in evil**

When the author first went to the Wilton Park Conference in 2004, he was of the view that the conference was about the archetypal discussion between good and evil: between the evil of nuclear weapons and the NWS that had them, on one hand, and the good of the NNWS who did not have them, on the other hand.

By 2014, however, he had realised that the battle of good and evil was actually taking place in the minds of just a few people within the NWS themselves. This internal mental battle, within these people, centred on this basic hypocrisy: we want to keep the weapons but we've committed ourselves to not having them. This point is central to later discussion.

Section 3:

Societal changes

Chapter 6:

The paradigm shift

During the conference the question was asked, to the effect of, "What is the next paradigm that could indicate the resolution of the problem?" The author responded, "The new paradigm is obvious, it's already here, it has been with us for some considerable time. Some 27 states have given up nuclear weapons and don't have any." These 27 states, like very many others, are prepared to operate in the positive trust of not having them. If the majority of states are able to live in this environment of not having them, why are the NWS not able to?

It is quite clear that this paradigm shift is already occurring, with the belief in the value of nuclear weapons receding fast.

What does a paradigm shift mean?

This is described more fully below, but it refers to a change in the basic assumptions that underpin societal belief and understanding in relation to the true nature of reality. Such a change in belief and understanding typically takes time to travel through society.

The belief in a flat Earth changed to a belief in a spherical Earth; in the same way Copernicus, alone as one person, voiced the opinion that the Earth went round the sun, instead of the sun going round the Earth. A belief change and a paradigm shift occurs as it moves from one person understanding a new truth to that truth travelling through the community until it is embraced by all.

Wikipedia describes the process this way: "When enough significant anomalies have accrued against a current paradigm, the scientific discipline is thrown into a state of *crisis*, according to Kuhn. During this crisis, new ideas, perhaps ones previously discarded, are tried. Eventually a *new* paradigm is formed, which gains its own new followers, and an intellectual 'battle' takes place between the followers of the new paradigm and the hold-outs of the old paradigm." Furthermore Wikipedia states, "Sometimes the convincing force is just time itself and the human toll it takes, Kuhn said" and summarises the colloquial term *paradigm shift* as, "simply the (often radical) change of worldview".

60-80% want nuclear disarmament

It is important to note that the populations of most countries – on opinion polls between 60% and 80% of the populations, including those of the NWS – want nuclear disarmament. It is quite clear that the doctrine of deterrence, which has always been held to be the reason for maintaining nuclear weapons, is now totally outdated, discredited and unsustainable: morally, legally and practically. This will be highlighted further below.

So where then, does the belief in the value of nuclear weapons still lie? Clearly, not amongst the majority of populations, who are putting pressure upon their politicians to get rid of them. The author's experience from questioning participants' beliefs at the conference is that it is essentially the senior military and the arms manufacturers who want to hang onto their nuclear "toys" and not give them up, even though many of their own senior colleagues have changed their beliefs: there are many ex-military servants who have publicly denounced the concept of deterrence and the continued existence of nuclear weapons.

Position of deterrence unsustainable

Diplomats, politicians and civil servants are visibly finding their positions increasingly unsustainable. Civil servants and government staffers have to play an uneasy policy game of having one foot in each camp – one to satisfy the public that they are "working towards" disarmament – and one to satisfy the official government position on the need to maintain nuclear weapons.

The UK (a NWS), in particular, despite considerable public pressure, declares the matter of nuclear weapons "settled". This means that the leaders of the major political parties have agreed that they are not going to discuss the matter anymore until they make a decision to renew the

Trident submarines in 2016. In other words, there is no room for argument and no room for the matter to be raised in the 2015 General Election. The matter is therefore hidden from further democratic discussion and debate. One can question, "why?" However, this position could well be challenged by the Scottish Nationalist Party, if it gains the balance of power in the UK elections; it is reported as saying, "nobody seriously believes that Scotland, a country of 5.25 million people, would want to be in possession of nuclear weapons. That would be a bad thing for Scotland."

The military and suppliers of arms

To reiterate, the belief in the value of nuclear weapons seems to remain principally in the minds of a few senior people in the military and suppliers of their arms, who have hijacked the thinking of a few government ministers and the democratic processes of the NWS (probably not least because of the vast amounts of money that move in the direction of the weapons manufacturers). In most circumstances, when the democratic process is hijacked by business interests for private monetary gain, this action is called corruption.

So what is necessary to change the belief in those minds? Even the President of the United States, in his Prague speech in 2009, did "state clearly and with conviction America's commitment to seek the peace and security of a world without nuclear weapons." If he wants to achieve that goal (rather than merely continue to "seek" it) surely he can make it happen – in his own words, "Yes we can!" He is supposedly the most powerful man on the planet – and in charge of by far the greatest number of nuclear weapons in any nation state. What is the problem, why "can't" he?

This book endeavours to travel deeper into this question in the following chapters.

Chapter 7:

The pressures on the Nuclear Weapons States

Reference has already been made to the Humanitarian Statement of October 2013 when New Zealand delivered to the UN General Assembly's First Committee a statement on behalf of 124 states expressing deep concern over the humanitarian impact of nuclear weapons.

This initiative is to demonstrate the growing momentum to address the nuclear weapons issue and the need for their elimination by focusing discussions on the humanitarian impacts. The key message from the experts and international organisations as part of that initiative was that, "No state or international body could address the immediate humanitarian emergency caused by a nuclear weapon detonation or provide adequate assistance to victims".

The key feature of this initiative has been the proposal to work towards an international treaty to prohibit nuclear weapons – a Nuclear Weapons Convention (NWC) – even, if necessary, without participation of the NWS.

Development of humanitarian law

Humanitarian law has been developing over the years to enable it to become a greater lever on the NWS. It is clear that the pressure to outlaw nuclear weapons is building, both from politicians and from non-governmental organisations around the world, and also from the wider populations of civil society, both within NNWS and NWS. There now exist a very large number of civil society groups working to put pressure upon the NWS to achieve nuclear disarmament.

Pressure is being brought to bear upon the hypocrisies and contradictions within the belief in deterrence and in the attempt to maintain nuclear weapons; those few people who believe in the concept of deterrence and the value of maintaining nuclear weapons are becoming like emperors without any clothes: their contradictions are visible to all, and are becoming increasingly unsustainable.

Why have we not seen World War III?

The best argument used by these proponents of deterrence at the conference is the fact that there has been no world war for the last 70 years; their argument is that the existence of nuclear weapons is responsible for this state of affairs. A more valid counter-argument is that it has been the presence of the United Nations, enabling discussions between potentially warring states, which has prevented World War III.

Wikipedia says, "World War III denotes a hypothetical successor to World War II, that is likely [to be] nuclear and devastating in nature...This war is anticipated and planned for by military and civil authorities... Concepts range from limited use of nuclear weapons to the destruction of the planet."

The belief that deterrence will fail

This description in itself indicates the biggest limitation of the belief in nuclear weapons as deterrence: the military are "anticipating and planning" for WWIII entirely on the basis of the use of nuclear weapons. This indicates that they themselves believe that deterrence will fail and that nuclear weapons will be used for WWIII.

Part of the argument for deterrence is, "It has been our defence policy for 70 years." There is no reason that it has to continue to be the defence policy of a few NWS; this can change in the twinkling of an eye. The argument that it has stopped world wars does not hold up to greater scrutiny. In the main it has been the NWS – supposedly responsible for peace and security in the world – that have been responsible for most of the recent major threats, attacks and invasions on other nation states.

A relic of the Cold War

Nuclear weapons are a relic from the Cold War, when

there was just a standoff between Russia and America, in the now also discredited concept of "the balance of powers". Nuclear Weapons are useless against the practical realities of current life. They were useless against the 9/11 attacks, they are useless against dealing with Non-State Actors (NSA) like ISIS. In fact, it is hard to imagine any situation now where they could be useful as part of a rational defence policy. At best it seems that their role is to give the nuclear NWS a belief that they are invincible, allowing them to act like bullies in attacking other countries around the world, but all this belief in invincibility does is set the belief up for challenge, by the likes of Osama bin Laden, Saddam Hussein, Iran, North Korea, and ISIS. What this illusory belief in invincibility does also is encourage other NNWS to acquire nuclear weapons.

NWS are not invincible

The evidence of events such as 9/11 shows clearly that the Nuclear Weapons States are not invincible, if only for the fact that most such attacks come from within. Indeed, many argue that the risks are moving much more towards cyber security now than physical security, and in this regard, nuclear weapons can have no value at all.

Chapter 8:

World domination

The NWS are currently transfixed by the perceived threat of world domination by Islam, against which nuclear weapons are useless. However, in the year 2000, the declared vision of the US Government was for "Full Spectrum Dominance": for the US to dominate the world across all sectors of governance.

Provoking a reaction

The author's response to the UK Strategic Defence Review at that time was that this self-serving vision was likely to provoke an alternative response to challenge that limited thinking. The response was not long in coming in the form of 9/11. The ISIS ideology is similar, best expressed as "our self-serving ideology is better than yours" or even perhaps the religious view: "There is only one God, but our God, not your God".

Collectively designed global leadership

The solution, of course, is not for world domination by any one nation state or group, but by a more sensible, and more effective, collectively designed system for global leadership and global decision-making. This could easily be designed to meet the common values and common needs of the world (and these can now easily be identified) without the need to resort to violence to settle differences of opinion.

The NWS are in prime position to help design and create such a new system of global leadership, together with the NNWS. This could be designed to be much more flexible for the future, instead of trying to continue with a now moribund system based upon the UN Security Council, still run, as designed 70 years ago to be unchangeable, by the victors of World War II.

Adapt or die

The rule now, in our rapidly changing world, is adapt or die. For the avoidance of doubt, the author is very motivated to pursue such a change project for a new form of global leadership. It is logical that such a project should begin where the greatest current source of global threat and power lies: to resolve the divide over nuclear disarmament.

Chapter 9:

National sovereignty and democracy

As discussed in the author's previous books, it is clear that in the majority of states, democracy does not really work nowadays. The forms of democracy were designed a long time ago and are much too crude to operate effectively in the current climate of instantaneous information transfer, whether via the internet or the media, with instant demands from global public opinion.

The electoral system is creaking and in many countries it doesn't work properly:

- The party system doesn't work very well.

- The choices of candidates are, in many cases,

invidious.

- The quality of candidates is often not very good.

- And perhaps the most insidious of all is that the influence of business continues to be a corrupting factor at the centre of most democracies, even though businesses do not have any votes within a democratic system.

Democracy needs a feedback system

A healthy democracy needs a healthy feedback system. Any system of control needs to have a feedback system so that an element of the output modifies the input to check that it is functioning properly and to stop it getting out of control. This does not happen in relation to nuclear weapons, where discussion is not permitted on the subject within the democratic process.

The idea that certain nation states should be able to retain the absolute autonomy and power to destroy life on the planet at the push of a button is now past its use by date. As made clear previously, the majority of global public opinion is against the idea.

The problem can be solved

What becomes obvious in relation to nuclear weapons is that the solution lies not in the disparate nation states working in isolation and opposition to each other on the threat of attack from each other, but in talking together to move on to solve the problem; after all, that's the central purpose of the United Nations.

Intentional vulnerability rather than illusory invincibility

But it seems that nation states, on this subject, at least, still have problems talking to each other. They would rather maintain, instead, the threats and the fears and the posturing, in their belief of their own invincibility. The concept of intentional vulnerability is a much better standpoint than the concept of invincibility, however, and it was 20 years ago that the author first came across this understanding, developed in the United States. It seems that it takes a long time for some understandings to propagate out to those who are in control of the nation states.

It is clear that in order to have useful discussions on the subject of disarmament, the NWS will need to understand the concept of intentional vulnerability and extend greater trust towards other states, in the way that the NWS already expect the NNWS to behave.

Transcending national sovereignty

It was to this end that the author co-founded the project for the United Nations Parliamentary Assembly, the concept of which has been supported by the three major trans-national parliaments: the European Parliament, the Latin American Parliament and the Pan-African Parliament – because the politicians who work on the world stage are very aware of the need to talk together and try and resolve the global problems which cannot be resolved at national level, within any one nation state.

The issue of nuclear weapons is the biggest global problem, on a similar standing with the issue of global warming; and beyond these two problems there is a long list of issues which cannot be handled at the level of the individual nation states and which need global discussion for global solutions. It is time for the world to move away from the concept of national sovereignty. Indeed, this move is already taking place in relation to the regional groupings of nations. The concept of national sovereignty is another outdated concept that needs to evolve into a transformed system of global governance.

It is easy to see that Nation States are simply historic boundary areas of administration. It makes no sense for these administrative areas to be threatening to fight each other, in the same way that it makes no sense for different counties or states within a country to have armies, nuclear weapons or to threaten to fight each other. Should Maine have nuclear weapons as a deterrent against a possible attack from New Jersey? Should Essex have nuclear weapons as a deterrent against Suffolk?

These ideas are as nonsensical as any nation states having nuclear weapons or fighting each other.

All of these growing perceptual changes will require the focus of attention to be shifted onto the meaning of trust, which will be discussed in a later chapter. After all, what is the trust level between Maine and New Jersey, or between Essex and Suffolk? It is high.

What is the trust level between NWS and NNWS? Low.

Section 4:

A step change

Chapter 10:

The transformation model for paradigm shift

At the conference a number of participants publicly expressed the belief that the purpose of diplomats was to reach a compromise. To the author this seems to be an extraordinarily low outcome to try to achieve. Compromise is generally a lose-lose outcome. Both parties give up something to compromise, both parties lose from where they started out. Both end up dissatisfied.

The possibility of true resolution

A much better place to aim for is the concept of resolution or reconciliation. Resolution is a concept where not only do both parties win but also they reach a superior place that they couldn't even see existed before. This happens through a process of transformation. Once they find themselves in this new place, they are filled with so much more energy and enthusiasm that they wonder why they hadn't got there a long time before – the solution seems obvious in retrospect. This is the process of transformation and involves a *change of state*.

A world full of resources

Surely in a process of seeking a solution, to the disarmament divide or any other global issue, one of the first prerequisites is to aim higher, is to aim for the best outcome that can possibly be achieved in the world. There is, after all, a world full of resources to support such a process.

The transformation process is a useful model for understanding such a process of change, and at the same time for speeding up a paradigm shift. The example of a paradigm shift that was given previously was the shift in belief, from the idea that the sun goes around the world, to the knowledge that the world goes around the sun. That was a change in global belief that could be identified back down to the initial understanding of one person, Copernicus, in the 1500s. He decided not to publish his findings widely because they were so clearly counter to current belief and he was concerned about the response. Many decades later, Galileo, now called "the father of modern science", picked up Copernicus' concept of heliocentrism. In 1616, he was ordered by the Pope "to abandon completely... the opinion that the sun stands still at the center of the world and the earth moves..." as contrary to Holy Scripture. Four months later, he was found "vehemently suspect of heresy" by the Inquisition and sentenced to house arrest for the rest of his life.

Hanging onto outdated belief

So in that example, it was the religious leaders of the time who hung onto the then outdated belief, because the change threatened their own belief and understanding, their teaching and their credibility. It was religious leaders of the time who held the greatest power and thought that it made them invincible.

What happens as belief change travels through society is that more and more people gain the understanding of a new truth until everybody accepts it as the current wisdom and indeed sees the new reality with their own eyes. This is best described by the phrase, "everything changes and yet nothing changes" – there is an *apparent* reversal in reality but, in fact, while everything changed in that new *understanding* of the reality, nothing *actually* changed in terms of the reality of the universe or the solar system.

A new understanding of reality

That new understanding of reality was completely incomprehensible to somebody in the old belief. The evidence previously was that the sun went around the Earth – it was written in the Holy Scripture, no less – so who could believe anything otherwise? Yet equally so, the old understanding of reality is now completely incomprehensible to somebody holding the new belief.

It is the same with the disarmament divide. The NWS hold their historic understanding that they must protect themselves from a perceived external threat of annihilation, but is this threat real or are they creating it themselves? Does it really exist or is it an illusion?

Hanging onto existing power

Who are the people hanging onto the last vestiges of the old belief? As mentioned earlier, they are those senior members of the military and the arms manufacturers who want to hang onto their own existing power and profits. They feel they would lose out if there were a final acceptance of the change in belief that is travelling the world. Paradoxically, however, like the religious leaders of old, if they could see the truth, and grasp the new reality, they are in a good position to drive the change through and stand to benefit more than anybody else, by being seen as true leaders rather than ostriches with their heads in the sand, or emperors without any clothes.

The possibility of leading the change

It is those people who are the equivalent of the religious

leaders of old and who are the most intransigent to the change of belief. It is in those people that the resistance is becoming greatest.

For example, in the UK, politicians are unable to discuss the matter. Why? Because they know that they cannot logically or emotionally maintain the arguments of old any longer. In this technologically fast-changing world, the leaders are those who understand change, embrace it and are at the forefront of change, whilst the fools are those who try to maintain the pretence of the old outdated belief. The UK in particular is well placed to switch from being a fool to a leader of the change.

That is transformation: when a belief change takes place, it can happen in the twinkling of an eye, in the mind of the beholder. The worldview changes and the understanding of reality changes. There is a reversal and a change of state. Energy is liberated and there is a new motivation. This transformation can happen for a person, a nation and a world. It can happen in an instant and does not need to take decades. The world of science and technology understands this and is charging ahead: contracts are placed to manufacture devices that have not yet been designed or created. In politics, however, the world is stuck in systemic beliefs that are hundreds of years old, such as, "This is the way we have always done it". So? It is time for the world of politics and governance to accept the new reality of rapid change and redesign.

It was noticeable at the conference, when the author tested the beliefs of certain people, how they would refuse to discuss their beliefs beyond a certain point. It was clear to both parties that those people knew that their arguments could no longer stand up to examination by outside society, and that they had lost the moral and intellectual supremacy. That is the territory of change and that is the territory of a new potential; that is where the point of transformation lies.

What happens in transformation?

In a transformation process, two opposing forces – two apparent opposites – come together; but instead of continuing to oppose each other, as in the old doctrine of a balance of power, and instead of finding a compromise, where they are both weakened, both of those forces are turned into a new direction and align themselves together in that new direction with the combined energy of both. The two forces have joined together in a new reality, in a different state, which is totally different from that which existed previously.

There are many examples of this happening. It is not a theoretical model, but is one that can be seen operating in other areas of science. An example, from chemistry, is that sodium and chlorine are two dangerous chemicals: dangerous to life, poisonous; yet when they combine – and there is an inherent tendency for them to want to combine – they become salt, which is an essential part of human diet.

Moreover, salt is in a very stable state; two dangerous, volatile and unstable elements come together into a new mode of stability, from which it is impossible for them to revert to their previous dangerous, volatile state. This is another classic outcome of transformation: a change of state; reality is no longer the same as it was before; the state of being has changed and there can be no going back.

A new identity has been created and much energy released in the process.

Potential for release of energy

There is the same potential in relation to the nuclear weapons disarmament divide. The opportunity exists for all of the various NWS to come together with the NNWS into a new state with a new purpose; and that new purpose would liberate the huge amount of energy, currently bound up in maintaining the old belief in the value of nuclear weapons. The amount of energy that would be liberated into the world would be commensurate with the amount of energy currently bound up in nuclear weapons: instead of being used to threaten the destruction of human life on the planet, it could be used to transform the state of human life on this planet.

To take a simple example, if all the money that was spent on nuclear weapons and defence was used for humanitarian purposes, life on this planet would indeed be transformed. Global expenditure on arms and defence is now annually over $1.7 trillion, whereas the cost of providing drinking water to everybody in the world has been estimated at about $12 billion; under 1% of the cost. It is the same with providing everybody with food, another $12 billion; also under 1%. It is just a matter of repositioning the resources. It could be easy to do.

So what would it take?

This would only take a change in belief within a few people. Extraordinary to contemplate really, isn't it? Just a change in belief in a very few people within the NWS and the desire of the world, embodied in the UN Charter, for disarmament – complete disarmament, note – could come about effortlessly.

The Role of the United Kingdom

One of the saddest things for the author as a UK citizen is that the UK could be the best state within the NWS to lead and make this change happen; and yet currently it is also one of the most intransigent. There are those in the political and governmental system who would disagree with that statement. They say, something like, "But we've reduced our power down to one Trident nuclear submarine at sea (out of four) with 16 missiles on it. That is the minimum capability it is realistic to have".

But one UK Trident nuclear missile has three independent warheads in it, and each warhead has 100 kilotons of power in it. The UK has some 200 warheads. The bomb that destroyed Hiroshima was about 13 kilotons. So the UK, having the least number of nuclear weapons in the P5, has around 1600 Hiroshimas in warheads. Even the destructive power of one Trident submarine is still huge – seemingly around 400 Hiroshimas – and yet those who insist on keeping Trident, try to belittle the vast power of these Weapons of Mass Destruction, which the P5 Member States insist that others should not be permitted to have.

Perhaps the UK military are comparing their missiles to the US missiles, each of which carry up to eight independently targetable warheads and each warhead having a yield of 475 kilotons, thus providing each *missile* with the destructive power of around 300 Hiroshima bombs. In comparison, a UK missile with the destructive power of "only" around 23 Hiroshima bombs seems like a poor relation – to the UK military, perhaps. But potential recipients of these UK missiles are likely to take a rather different view.

Majority do not want nuclear weapons

Like the majority of the public, and as a UK voter, the author does not support the threat of even the UK level of "minimal" destruction of 1600 Hiroshima disasters being carried out in his name: not even the threat, let alone the prospect of accidental action. Without any public risk assessment or control, the UK could, by itself, accidentally initiate global nuclear war. This is the kind of leverage UK citizens do not need.

In 2006 Prime Minister Tony Blair told MPs that it would be "unwise and dangerous" for the UK to give up its nuclear weapons. By then the PM was no stranger to "unwise and dangerous" decisions himself. His statement should, more logically, have been that it would be "unwise and dangerous" for the UK to keep them – indeed "unwise and dangerous" for the entire world if the UK kept them.

The process starts with trust

If the UK Government's view is that its capability is so small, it is equally a short step towards getting rid of it. It is obvious that neither the UK nor the world would be changed materially if the UK gave up its nuclear missiles, so why hang onto them? That one act might of course result in all of the other NWS giving up theirs, too. This whole process needs to start with trust: with a demonstration of trust and an extension of trust. The UK could be the first of the NWS to take the small step to complete nuclear disarmament: its weapons serve no useful purpose, but they carry a huge cost burden.

Instead of renewing the Trident system at £26bn ($40bn), the UK alone could provide the whole world with a proper system of drinking water and food distribution ($24bn) and save over one third of the money. Which is the better decision for the world?

It is both a small step and a big step to take: a change in belief, a change of mind, a change of heart, a change of understanding. It can happen in the twinkling of an eye.

After all, most people – and most nation states – already have that understanding; they have made the paradigm shift; only relatively few people remain with their heads in the sand, pretending that the old reality still exists. They hold the key to transformation.

Chapter 11:

Beyond belief: the healing process

This report has already highlighted the area of the hypocrisy within the NWS and also the apparent paradox embodied within the NWS: that they have both committed to giving up nuclear weapon WMDs and yet still want to keep them. This hypocrisy is reflected within the NPT because the Treaty has now become indefinite, so there is no time pressure to make the change. This hypocrisy is also reflected in the Prague speech of President Obama, with his assertion that America is committed to "a world without nuclear weapons", and yet, "but perhaps not in my lifetime".

Even more paradoxically, he went on to say next, that, "We, too, must ignore the voices who tell us that the world cannot change. We have to insist, 'Yes we can'." So the

President is clearly rather confused about the matter: he says America and he are committed to change, saying "yes we can", and to ignoring the voices that say "no we cannot", yet he also says "perhaps not in my lifetime". The latter caveat simply confirms that he does not believe he can and is not actually committed to the change. It provides no certainty of change, only the prospect of no change.

Paradox becomes hypocrisy

There are people trying to hold these two different positions at the same time; "we will and we won't", and trying to rationalise that to the rest of the world. So what starts off as a paradox – where there are seemingly two opposing truths existing at the same time – moves into hypocrisy, saying one of them but doing the opposite, or saying both and doing one. A paradox is not a stable state; it is rather like the sodium and the chlorine, the two different ideas need to combine within the human mind. The human mind is not designed for holding two opposing ideas for too long.

At the conference the idea was expressed that the mark of a professional was to be able to hold two opposing concepts in the mind at the same time. This was a strange new idea to the author. For, in reality, such a position cannot be held for long. It is not a stable sustainable position. Like sodium and chlorine put together: if two opposites are held together in one mind, the mind is compelled to resolve the matter into a different state. If a person tries to maintain two opposing positions, that person is most likely to end up with a split personality, or cognitive dissonance; the end result could be psychosis, schizophrenia, the holder could become a psychopath. It is not a holistically healthy state. That is why hypocrisy is so common: it is an easier way round the problem.

We know how to resolve it

This dilemma seems rather too true with some of the NWS; but we know how to resolve this. We need to work our way back to the origin of the problem: to resolve the opposing beliefs. To do that we go beyond the two existing beliefs into a third belief, which transcends the other two.

This takes us back to the model of transformation.

The reason it is difficult to hold two opposing beliefs in the mind is because it consumes so much energy. As in external reality, the opposing beliefs tend to fight each other in the mind. Their energy needs to be integrated, it needs to be resolved and it needs to be directed in a different direction – with a new purpose. The problems that appear "out there" in reality need to be resolved within the minds of those attempting to hold the paradox and instead living the hypocrisy.

Parallels in physical healing

The healing process in general relies very much on belief – someone holding the understanding of a transformed belief. It is not just "faith healing" that relies on belief: people believe in the superior understanding of the doctor or even the efficacy of drugs and medication.

This idea of belief is not well understood in traditional medicine, in the same way as it is not understood in the world of politics, but within these models we have the ability to transform the way we run our world, just by going beyond current belief to a resolved, healed, state. We know how to do this and we need to get on and do it.

These understandings have been around for many years. It is time they got through to the decision makers in governments.

An addiction

Another way of looking at the disarmament divide is through the concept of addiction. The NWS are like heroin addicts who came across an opportunity that appeared to them to give them a benefit. They knew that the rest of the world thought that the opportunity to get involved with hard drugs was a crazy way to go, that would ultimately harm them very seriously and possibly everyone else as well, but that didn't bother them. They got in deeper, justified their position and their need to themselves. Their addiction indeed impinged upon, and upset, everyone around them.

They started telling lies to their friends and to the rest of the world. Yet their self-destructive behaviour was always clearly obvious to everyone else – from the start. They became real pains for the rest of the world, attacking others, on false pretences, to steal their resources. Eventually, though, the truth started to dawn: that they would need serious help and determination, to extract themselves from their damaging self-imposed predicament, and to rejoin the rest of the world.

As the saying goes, "Power corrupts and absolute power corrupts absolutely".

The same is true of WMDs.

It really is time for the NWS to turn themselves in for voluntary detox and to change their beliefs and behaviours: to turn away from the MAD idea of Mutually Assured Destruction and to see the light of redemption. It only takes a decision, after all.

In the minds of men...

In the Constitution of UNESCO – the United Nations

Educational, Scientific and Cultural Organisation – signed in 1945, the first line says:

"The Governments of the States Parties to this Constitution on behalf of their peoples declare:

"That since wars begin in the minds of men, it is in the minds of men that the defences of peace must be constructed;

"That ignorance of each others ways and lives has been a common cause, throughout the history of mankind, of that suspicion and mistrust between the peoples of the world through which their differences have all too often broken into war..."

The desire for the world to live in peace has always been present and remains present. Yet only now, in this age of the internet, does the world have all the necessary understandings, ability and resources, to come together to connect and cooperate to truly achieve peace.

This can be achieved simply by changing remarkably few

minds: the emperors who wear no clothes. They, themselves, now know who they are and that they have a clear choice. They could get together to build themselves still higher defences to protect their beliefs from an inevitable eventual change, or they could just decide to join a greater process for detox and a rapid and painless recovery. How much longer must the rest of the world suffer from the consequences of these few remaining addicts?

War no longer boosts popularity

What many leaders have not yet noticed is that, since 2000, war no longer boosts the popularity of leaders. Now that people can see, via the internet, the awful truth on the other side of a war, they rightly blame their leaders, as the sole individuals responsible for the war, for causing the suffering to the population on the receiving end, who can do nothing to end the war. The people can now see the dreadful insanity of their leaders in deciding to go to war, by seeing the consequences. It is time for leaders to give up their addiction to war as a response to differences of opinion.

The Post-2015 Agenda

2015 is the year for the UN General Assembly to decide upon the "Post-2015 Development Agenda". The primary response from consultation meetings and documents relating to the Post-2015 Agenda was that more than anything else, the people of the world wanted to stop violence and war. Why? Because where there is violence and war, there is no prospect of any other form of development. The painful disabling effect of war and violence – and the inability of those suffering from it to stop it – is similar to the way a person suffering from severe pain is unable to focus on, or attend to, anything else, until healing has occurred.

Yet the proposed UN Post-2015 Agenda does not include much reference to this necessity to deal first with ending violence and war. Why not? Because violence and war is a matter for the UN Security Council. Therefore the primary future development agenda for the United Nations will be largely disabled and rendered ineffective by the problems with the Security Council. It is time that the UN General Assembly dispensed with the disabling pain of the Security Council. It has the power to do so.

The world needs to reclaim its power over its own pain, in the same way that it needs to integrate its Jungian shadow. Giving our power away to an "other" body leads to separation and conflict. Reclaiming our power is the road to resolution and a transformed state.

Chapter 12:

The development of trust

The way to end the use of war as a method of resolving differences of opinion, is the way to peace, connection and love. These three values have long been established as the highest desires of mankind. The way is very simple: it involves telling the truth – and this leads to trust. Lies lead the way to disputes, to violence, war, hatred and division.

It is hard work to fight wars, to maintain lies, to hide things. One risks being found out and the truth being discovered, and the only way to maintain that position is to isolate oneself from challenge and questioning, such as the challenges that come from the media, for example. The media sometimes sees its purpose as being to uncover lies and hypocrisy. In London, Fleet Street used to be called "The Street of Shame" because the aim of newspapers was to show up hypocrisy and lies.

Hypocrisy, of course, falls within the category of telling lies: saying one thing, doing another, no congruence, no match, no truth or trust in the system, the organisation or the person.

Hypocrisy, for example, is saying a nation stands for freedom and then imprisoning people without trial. It is saying a nation is peace-loving and then invading other nations. It is being pro-life and subscribing to the Ten Commandments (including "Thou shalt not kill") and then killing over 100,000 people. There are endless examples of hypocrisy in politics. Hypocrisy kills both truth and trust.

The way to resolve disputes is to focus on the common understanding of truth, which often means the common underlying fear. This involves trust.

Trust is essential

What is trust and how does one grow it? One has to start by telling the truth and by trusting those who were not previously trusted. To some people, this doesn't seem a very sensible route, as it involves risk. However, trust is about confidence in the truth. If one is confident in the truth of one's position, one is more able to trust that position than if one is not confident in the truth of that position. Truth and trust in reality reduce risk and increase security – and freedom.

What is the situation with regard to the NPT and trust? The NNWS are confident in their truth. They are committed to disarmament. They are committed to trusting each other and indeed trusting the NWS to maintain their side of the bargain, not to attack them, and to achieve disarmament.

But where is the trust in the NWS? The reason for having nuclear weapons is an extreme lack of trust in others and this lack of trust can be seen without exception in all of the current NWS. As highlighted before, these are the states most likely to generate hostilities and go to war on other nation states, from the illusory sense of invincibility gained by possession of nuclear weapons. Iran is proving to be a focus for the NWS's lack of trust – and it is bringing a focus to the hypocrisy in the NPT itself.

Lack of trust within the NWS

Even more importantly, one must ask where is the lack of trust in the NWS? It is known that the majority of the populations within the NWS do not want nuclear weapons and want disarmament. But their Governments do not deliver disarmament. So the people do not trust their Governments. It is, after all, the weapons manufacturers who manufacture the distrust in the NWS, and who convince their Governments to keep supplying them with money to manufacture weapons and, consequently, distrust. It is the nuclear weapons manufacturers who are the real problem in this terrible "game". It is they who lean upon the military, who lean upon the governments to keep the game running.

But it is becoming clearer that time is running out for this outdated nuclear war game. In the same way that Scotland questions its role as repository of the UK's nuclear weapons, there is a movement in the USA to question the $5bnpa nuclear weapons role and purpose of the US National Labs (see www.reinventors.net). One suggestion is to repurpose the National Security Labs as a Global Security Centre: as a network node for common global security problems, along with more enlightened global (rather than national) approaches for dealing with global problems.

Even outside the NWS, in a nation such as Germany, an NNWS which has nuclear weapons on its soil but is not in control of them, this insane hypocrisy is becoming harder to bear. It is not surprising that politicians and governments are not trusted!

Weapons are a reflection of fear

The very fact of holding nuclear weapons is a huge statement about the lack of trust that a nation state has in itself and in others. Indeed, any weapons are only held because of the fear within the psyche of those who hold them, whether an individual or a nation state. The majority of people in the world do not need weapons; they trust the world around them. It is only those who do not trust who need weapons. Surely it is time to start extending trust and developing trust rather than continuing to develop weapons.

In this discussion of trust, it is essential to take note of the book by Stephen M. R. Covey, "The Speed of Trust", which gives one of the best models currently available of how to develop trust. The strap-line of the book is that Trust is: "The One Thing that Changes Everything".

The loss of trust

Covey says, "when people are trusted, they become inspired and don't need control". Yet the knee-jerk reaction of many states is to increase control of their populations, rather than extend trust. It is currently fashionable to pass vast government sums (secretly) into security services to increase surveillance and control of populations. The UK, for example, is reported to have around 10% of the world's security cameras, for its 1% of the world's population. It used to be communist Russia that was decried for this "big brother" surveillance of its population. The UK Government still trumpets that its internet surveillance is "fully in accordance with the law", whilst knowing full well that there are deliberately big holes in the law which allow the security services the freedom to do what they want.

This is not the way for Governments and politicians to build trust. Are they bothered? Seemingly not. But they need to be, because the world is changing very fast. Political systems around the world are no longer fit for purpose in the internet age of instant response. In the UK, a recent voter survey surprised politicians by finding that voters were not apathetic but angry. Well, not very surprising! This results from the increasing destruction of trust, present in the UK, but more articulate in the Arab Spring, ISIS & ISIL. Nuclear weapons are not much use against dissatisfied electorates.

The model of trust

Covey's models are layered. He indicates that the different "waves" of trust are:

1. Self Trust: the Principle of Credibility (with 4 cores of credibility)

2. Relationship Trust: the Principle of Behaviour (with 13 behaviours)

3. Organisational Trust: the Principle of Alignment

4. Market Trust: the Principle of Reputation

5. Societal Trust: the Principle of Contribution

Even without much discussion of Covey's model, it should be clear from the words, Credibility, Behaviour, Alignment, Reputation and Contribution, that these are areas where politicians, political leaders, parties and governments do not score very highly – in fact, usually abysmally – for voters. So there is no trust.

But Covey has an even more useful model; it is a matrix that plots propensity to trust against analysis, providing four variants:

1. Gullibility: High trust, low analysis

2. Judgement: High trust, high analysis

3. Indecision: Low trust, low analysis

4. Suspicion: Low trust, high analysis

It is quite clear from the previous observations (according to opinion polls) that most politicians and governments around the world operate in a climate of low trust. Depending upon how analytical they are (whether as individuals or as governments), this will place them in a position of either "indecision" or "suspicion". Neither of these positions is a very good place to be, but neither is "gullibility": the best place is in the "judgement" position.

Covey indicates that "suspicion" is the worst place to be because not only is there no trust, but also suspicion provokes adverse consequences. A suspicious mind looks for nasty things and generally has its expectations of nastiness fulfilled. Put another way, people who believe that the world is dangerous are likely to generate a more dangerous world for themselves, whereas people who believe that the world is benign will have a much easier life in the more benign world they create.

Lives by the sword, dies by the sword

The traditional phrase for this is, "He who lives by the sword, dies by the sword". It's the same perceptual result that one gets when one buys a new car and suddenly notices that there are lots of other ones of the same model driving around: what we focus on tends to grow. If we focus on fear and threat, fear and threat tend to grow, whilst if we focus on truth and trust, those tend to grow instead.

It should have become obvious to the reader that all of the nuclear weapons states, whether inside or outside the NPT, fall into the category of "suspicion": their strong, volatile, adverse expectations generate exactly the unwelcome consequences against which they are trying to protect themselves. This an extremely foolish form of behaviour, especially for the P5, which are charged with maintaining peace and security in the world, but which generate the exact opposite response by their suspicious attitudes and behaviour.

Global peace and security clearly lies in extending

common trust, not in extending fear and threats and suspicion. The United Nations, with its inclusive and consensus behaviour, was designed to build trust. However, the P5, in their continuing control and behaviour on the UN Security Council, instead build suspicion, isolation and distrust: the exact opposite of their required role. It is not surprising that the United Nations, and the UN Security Council in particular, are falling ever more deeply into public distrust and disrepute.

Rebuilding trust in politics

Trust breaks down with lies and hypocrisy, saying one thing and doing another. This is the very embodiment of the global political system. Covey describes "politics" (as the world currently operates) and "trust" as opposites. As already indicated, opinion polls around the world show that on the scale of trust, politicians are at the bottom level, below all other professions.

But Covey also goes on to say that trust can be rebuilt and restored, and this can be done by extending trust; the solution is to trust first and get the results afterwards. And as said before, one trusts by knowing that one has the greater truth underneath, so that trust is not without foundation.

Quoting Covey again, after trust comes verification. "Trust and verify"; or in the words of an Arab proverb, "Trust in God and tie down your camel".

Verification under the NPT

It is noticeable how in the NPT regime there is a lot of focus on verification by the NWS amongst the NNWS. There is increasing attention and development of systems for improved verification as to whether or not there are fissile materials being used and in what form. There are increasing regimes to control the distribution of fissile materials; but it is also noticeable how none of this verification is applied to the NWS.

The author asked one high-ranking member in the military of one NWS as to when that state was going to open itself up to verification and inspection of its nuclear weapons and locations. The answer was silence – there could not be any answer – only hypocrisy.

Another effect of this hypocrisy appears in the fact that the NWS expect to be allowed to control the NNWS, but not be controlled themselves. Operating out of suspicion and control they expect the worst. They try to control against getting the worst and instead get what they expect. Covey recommends instead operating with trust and verification – expecting the best and just checking that that is what is actually happening, correcting if it is not. The answer is not to put the verification first; the answer is to put trust first, based upon truth, and the verification after. Yet the NWS do want to open themselves up to any verification inspections by outside parties: they are too distrustful.

This behaviour urgently needs to change. It is the presence of nuclear weapons as WMDs within the NWS that is feeding the breakdown of trust in the world and the consequent breakdown in peace and security: nuclear weapons are the primary cause and need to be eliminated – urgently – and a better system of global leadership established. As a world, we know how to do this, so let's get on with it. This project is more urgent and more useful

– and potentially quicker even - than putting a man on the moon.

Covey says:

"When trust is sufficient, laws are unnecessary; but when trust is insufficient, laws are unenforceable."

Section 5:

The move away from violence

Chapter 13:

Degeneration into violence and war – and out again

Whilst this ground has already been referred to, to some extent, in this report, it is worth reiterating that the route to violence and war is a fairly simple, well-worn path. It starts off with a difference of opinion based upon a difference of belief, which gives a difference of position on any given matter. Trust is the first thing to break down. Differences grow into disputes, which grow into arguments; then resentment builds and festers. At some point it becomes frustration that nothing is being resolved and then, if that lack of resolution continues, it turns into anger, then violence and then can turn into war.

The way to move away from violence and war is to tackle

the difference of belief that was the cause of the problem. One way to do that is by de-escalating back down through all of those stages: de-escalating the war into a temporary cessation of violence, albeit with angry feelings, etc. Alternatively one can set up a process where one can build trust between the parties, get them to come together and talk together with a facilitator who can see beyond their current problems. It is common to try to do both at the same time.

A different level of thinking

Einstein said that problems can never be resolved with the same level of thinking that created them. They need to be resolved at a different level.

Those with the problems need to be in the presence of someone who can see beyond those problems to the possibility of transformation beyond current belief.

Resolution of opposing beliefs comes through getting to the common truth behind those beliefs. That is often found to be the common fear that underlies the difference of position and the difference of belief: the two parties fighting typically will both have the same fear and yet will have come to two different, opposite conclusions as to ways of trying to resolve that fear.

This being the case, the solution lies, not in addressing the differences, but in addressing the common factors: the underlying truth, the underlying fear. These underlying factors are topics upon which opposing parties can start to agree.

As stated earlier, one of the things that the author highlighted in the conference, was that a common factor amongst the people attending was frustration – quite palpable frustration. That frustration indicated the common ground between the parties, showing up the fact that they were both looking for a point of resolution of the problems but couldn't find it.

The way to resolution

The purpose of this book is to build belief in the way in which the resolution can be found and built upon, in order to remove the most major tensions in the world.

What often happens in compromise solutions, where one party wins the war and the other party loses, is that there is no learning. One belief trumps another one, but actually the winning side does not move on, the winner just proves to itself, for example, its belief that weapons are the way forward. Therefore they feel justified in making ever more powerful weapons.

With true resolution comes learning

It is only through true resolution between the two parties that one gets the learning or the change in understanding, which enables them to move to the win-win situation and beyond it to higher understanding. It is at this point that there is a great release in energy and the parties can move forward in a new direction with a new trust, new aligned purpose in a new common state, to greater common contribution, with that reversal of understanding from their previous position.

This is not rocket science, but even if it were, the world

has sufficient understanding of rocket science. We've moved way beyond rocket science now; it's no longer the epitome of our understanding. The territory discussed here is the next level of understanding to which the world needs to move.

The NUCLEAR WAR Game

Chapter 14:

NPT morality and legality

For this chapter the author is indebted to Robert Green and his book "Security without Nuclear Deterrence". It is worth extracting some of the key points he makes. The author trusts that Commander Green and his publishers will not mind the use of these extracts, which are included as fair review to work to the same end. For further expansion it is essential to read his book. The author has selected some summary points, from the chapter on "Morality and Legality", as follows:

- "Nuclear deterrence entails a fundamental moral deception: using the most immoral means imaginable to achieve what governments of nuclear states claim are their highest moral ends."

- "Another intrinsic, inescapable part of the nuclear deterrence dogma is the generation of hostility and mistrust. By inhibiting cooperation in promoting true security; nuclear deterrence tends to be self-perpetuating. This adds another layer of deception, deepening the immorality further."

- "The basis of deterrence is living by threats. ... In the real world the laws that govern our conduct as citizens of civilised societies forbid the employment of threats and menaces in our interaction with one another."

- "The insulation of the armed forces and citizenry of the NWS from any moral or ethical concerns regarding the use of nuclear weapons is crucial if the nuclear deterrence doctrine is to retain its influence."

- "Any plea that such plans are designed to deter an 'evil force' is vitiated by the inescapable nature of nuclear weapons. As confirmed by Judge Mohammed Bedjaoui, President of the International Court of Justice, when it gave its advisory opinion on the legal status of the threat or use of nuclear weapons in July 1966, nuclear weapons are the 'ultimate evil'."

- There is reference to Pope Benedict asserting in his 2006 New Year message that, "the idea that nuclear weapons contribute to security was 'completely fallacious' ".

- "What has been happening recently is that for the first time the law and public opinion were harnessed on a moral issue centred on human rights."

- "The International Court of Justice (ICJ) cited the uniquely appalling characteristics of nuclear weapons: 'in particular their destructive capacity, their capacity to cause untold human suffering and their ability to cause damage to generations to come'. Indeed, it added that only nuclear weapons 'have the potential to destroy all civilisation and the entire ecosystem of the planet'."

- "Following the 1998 UK Strategic Defence Review, each UK Trident missile carried only three warheads, each of about 100 kilotons, but that was still the explosive power of 24 Hiroshima bombs."

- Commander Green refers to the importance of the

Nuremburg Charter and says, "the whole point of the Nuremburg Charter is that individuals, and especially leaders in war, should not be able to hide behind the state when taking decisions that might breach the principles and rules of international humanitarian law". He points out that under "Nuremburg Principle III: The fact that a person who committed an act, which constitutes a crime under international law, acted as Head of State or responsible government official does not relieve him from responsibility under international law."

- The [International] Court's expressed ruling was "the threat or use of nuclear weapons will generally be contrary to the rules of international law applicable in armed conflict and in particular the principles and rules of humanitarian law."

- In relation to the public who are opposing nuclear weapons, Commander Green says, "they are tapping into a deep and growing awareness that they are on the right side of morality, common sense, the law and public opinion."

- The ICJ's position on the illegality of the use of nuclear weapons under humanitarian law "has serious implications for all those involved in planning and deploying nuclear forces. In particular military professionals need to be seen to act within the law. This is the crucial difference between them and hired killers or terrorists."

- "Political will must be generated to persuade the governments to comply with the law, morality and common sense."

In conclusion, it can be seen that this covers a similar line of thinking as outlined within this report. Commander Green served in the military; his book provides a very useful and comprehensive analysis of the doctrine of nuclear deterrence.

Values, principles and standards

Underpinning morality and legality lies another territory where politicians fear to tread: the territory of values, principles and standards. Before any decision-making can be carried out in a consistent manner – rather than the usual adhoc, knee-jerk, inconsistent manner of politics – there must be common agreement upon the global basis for decision-making. It is very common for assumptions to be made about the basis for decision making, when it fact the basis has not been discussed and agreed upon.

The reason why this territory is so often avoided is because is it seen as the domain of religious belief. It is not surprising that there are tensions between, say, Christianity, Judaism and Islam, because the underlying values, principles and standards for decision-making and law-making are not properly discussed in our current system of global governance.

Experience shows that if sufficient time is spent in a process of discussion to explore and reach agreement upon common values, principles and standards, instead of leaving these to assumption, then common agreement and understanding can usually be reached. If this time is not spent on this territory, then disputes and differences of opinion are inevitable. These, of course, can ultimately lead to violence and war.

UK politicians, for example, will often refer to "British Values", without ever attempting to explain what these are. Probably most British people would assume that "freedom of speech" and "telling the truth" were important British values. Yet it is quite clear now that this is not the case. These concepts have been outlawed in much recent legislation, much of it under the guise of anti-terrorist legislation.

People are afraid to speak the truth

The concept of political correctness is now endemic in the UK, because people are afraid to speak the truth in case they inadvertently commit a criminal act. There are now so many vague "catch all" criminal laws that people no longer know what they are allowed to say, do, photograph, write, read (especially on the internet), or even think, without inadvertently committing a criminal offence or creating suspicion. Even writing a report like this might possibly be interpreted as anti-state (and anti current Government belief) and found to be contrary to some criminal legislation.

Why are such examples important in a discussion on global security? Because they illustrate ways in which governments do not consider the core values, principles and standards that are critically important as a foundation for decision-making and law-making. The result is that truth is repressed, along with the expression of it, with the further consequence that trust is destroyed and divisions and tensions increase – and security decreases.

The terrorist threat in the UK, as determined by MI5 Security Service, is currently at the level of "severe" (meaning: "an attack is highly likely"), being one level below the top level of "critical" (meaning: "an attack is expected imminently"). What does this mean in practice for the population? Absolutely nothing: it has no useful meaning to the public in terms of action or response.

It is interesting to note, in the context of this report, that the UK Government provides this seemingly useless and imprecise assessment of a terrorist attack (without defining terrorist, location or timing of attack or potential consequences), but does not provide other important risk assessments, such as the probability of an aircraft crash on

London or, even more importantly, the risk of an accidental nuclear weapons attack on the UK from another state.

Such Government risk assessments could be much more specific, as the numbers of aircraft are known and the numbers of armed nuclear weapons and missiles are known, along with the potential target locations and the more predictable consequences. Why are these risk assessments not provided by the UK and other Governments?

The sole purpose of the terrorist threat designation appears to be to spread a feeling of fear and insecurity amongst the population in order to justify increasing the "anti-terrorism" funding for the security services, rather than to provide any information useful to the public. There is little incentive for the Security Services to lower the stated risk level.

Governments use control, not trust

The road to repression for governments is easy.

Governments tend to focus upon control and the repression of truth and dissent, rather than upon building trust. Possession of nuclear weapons is that ultimate level of attempt at control. Possession of nuclear weapons is also therefore the ultimate level of destruction of trust in the world.

Governments, like businesses that try to control, do not like feedback: they see it as criticism and attack, rather than as valuable information to improve customer service and well-being. But then whole political processes, like legal processes, are designed to be adversarial, and they therefore build acrimony, rather than trust.

The route to real global security

The ultimate goal in the alternative route of extending and building trust is to unravel tensions and differences and so reach empathy and the ultimate connection of humanity between people where we experience unity. This is the route to real global security. Possession of nuclear weapons destroys the prospect of empathy as surely as the weapons themselves can destroy humanity. They keep the world in an ultimate state of insecurity.

Those who profess belief in the value of nuclear weapons have lost touch with what is really valuable in the world: real security, which is based upon truth, trust, empathy and common humanity.

Chapter 15:

Moving the disarmament

process forward

So how might all this discussion be turned into action? The obvious critical factor in all this is the need for the NWS – all of the NWS note, both within the NPT and outside it – to begin discussions together to address their common fears and the common underlying truth about their fear of each other. They need to do this in a structured process rather than just political posturing; but it needs to be done sensitively. How can this be possible? How might it be done?

The thrust of the previous material in this book is to illustrate that disarmament is a very important process and "why" it needs to happen. Now we look at "how" it might happen: we look at the first possible steps.

P5 are used to talking to each other

Let's look at the positions of the various NWS. The P5 – that is, the five NWS within the NPT: the USA, Russia, China, France and the UK – are all quite used to talking to each other. They may not be very civil sometimes and in particular in the current context, where the USA has signed yet further sanctions against the USSR, it is not surprising that there is not much cordial conversation going on between those two states. However, their difference can also be a point of opportunity to bring the two states together, for example in the USA agreeing to lift sanctions in return for co-operation on this matter and as a reward for better behaviour.

There may not currently be an agreed position between the five NWS but at least the three within NATO – the USA, France and the UK – can very easily have further discussions on this subject; and it has already been highlighted why the UK could become a leader in these discussions. Clearly the US is already somewhat onboard from the indications of the Prague speech. France is having its own economic problems, so may well appreciate being relieved of the economic burden of nuclear weapons.

The UK has signalled that it is going to make a decision on the future of Trident in 2016. The cost of this has been forecast to be £26 billion so progress towards disarmament is an opportunity to save that amount of money by not proceeding with the renewal of Trident and instead spending the money more wisely.

China's driving force is to seek harmony in the world and in international relations. China gives the impression of secretly despairing at the behaviour of other members of the P5. It is not difficult to envisage that it may well come onboard if there is a visible movement to improve trust.

The other nuclear powers

The main question is what to do about the powers outside the NPT Treaty – that is Israel, North Korea, Pakistan and India.

Israel prefers to take a position of even greater secrecy by not revealing whether or not it has nuclear weapons, although it is generally believed to have some. This creates an opportunity to declare for disarmament. Having already taking the position of not indicating whether or not it has nuclear weapons, it would be easy for Israel to take the position that it hasn't. If, in the process, it gained more reassurance about a reduction in the risks from its immediate neighbours, then this would no doubt help. Of course Israel is already very closely aligned with the USA.

North Korea has already indicated that it wants to be recognised as a nuclear weapon nation state, and that it wants to be a recognised "member of the club". So the prospect of gaining that recognition is likely to encourage it to enter discussions.

India and Pakistan seem to be playing their own game of escalating the threats and competing with one another. It wouldn't seem very difficult to dismantle this bipartisan escalation, especially given the USA's nuclear relations with India. The answer may lie in Kashmir.

The first important step that comes to mind is to invite the non-NPT NWS into the NPT club. This can be done either by creating a committee outside of the NPT or it can be done by bringing them within the NPT.

How might these conversations be established and operated? The answer is not for the author to impose here: it is a question of private discussions to find out in detail what each state's bottom-line fears are; but in practice, discussions between all states already take place and, as the saying goes, "when there's a will there's a way". Moving on the NPT and the disarmament process is the important factor.

Political will is already there

Political will is often seen as something that needs to take a long time to build, but in this situation political will is already there. The author has illustrated earlier how the great majority of the world wants to see disarmament. Political will is out there, in practice only relatively few people prevent it being effective.

The NPT is not likely to work effectively with four nuclear

weapon powers remaining outside of its remit and discussions. Some pride will have to be swallowed, perhaps, and some decisions, currently seen as "unacceptable" decisions, made about recognising the four powers outside the NPT – recognising them as NWS to be brought into discussion under the NPT banner. This needs to be done not by coercion but through a trust building process. If a belief is there that it could work then there's a great likelihood that it will work. And on the contrary, if the belief is there that it will not work, there's a certainty that it won't work.

So the first challenge for the NPT meeting in April 2015 is to decide to engage the four nuclear weapon powers currently outside the NPT and bring them within the NPT as NWS. This is essential. The second challenge is for an agreement within the NPT framework that it is possible to move rapidly towards further nuclear disarmament and a verification process for all NWS. The current position of the P5 NWS is that they are against the idea of a Nuclear Weapons Convention, yet it can be seen from the Humanitarian Initiative process that the Nuclear Weapons Convention may well happen regardless of the position of the NWS. The sooner the NWS adjust themselves to the renewed reality that is closing in on them the better. A change in belief can happen very quickly – indeed, it needs to happen quickly – and it need not be a painful process.

Turning resignation into optimism

2015 could be a very auspicious year: if the common sense of frustration between the NNWS & NWS is turned into a common motivation, the sense of resignation about the NPT review conference in April 2015 could be turned into optimism – that disarmament agreement could be reached very quickly. There is no need to be pessimistic; one needs to believe that a miracle can happen, taking the best positive reading of President Obama's Prague speech.

Mission statements

In this context it is worth referring to President Kennedy's mission statement to put a man on the moon. On 25 May 1961 President Kennedy said to Congress: "I believe that this nation should commit itself to achieving the goal, before this decade is out, of landing a man on the moon and returning him safely to earth". He didn't live very long (until November 1963) and didn't personally see that mission through, but it was achieved, nevertheless, in July 1969: in eight years the USA had put a man on the moon. Kennedy's mission statement embodied certainty: to achieve the specific goal by the end of the decade.

It should be easier than this for the world to come to a decision about disarmament of nuclear weapons and to turn it into verifiable reality. Again, how long is it necessary to take to change the belief? No time at all.

Comparing President Obama's Prague speech with President Kennedy's speech, what is the difference? President Obama's speech in Prague was, again, "I state clearly and with conviction America's commitment to seek the peace and security of a world without nuclear weapons. I am not naïve; the goal will not be reached quickly, perhaps not in my lifetime".

He's saying that he has conviction about the commitment, but at the same time he's indicating a great lack of conviction by saying, "perhaps not in my lifetime". As any businessman would know, a mission statement with a doubt built into it, which undermines it, is not very likely to be achieved, certainly not very quickly, as President Obama says.

Finding common ground

Why did the President put that caveat in? Perhaps to try to appease those members in the Republican Party who might otherwise have been worried by the speech. Perhaps then the place to start for the USA is to resolve the acrimonious relationship between the parties in Congress, especially regarding this issue. In fact there may be more common ground between the two parties on this matter than meets the eye – that possibility is certainly worth exploring.

So what needs to be agreed between the NWS? After all, it only needs to be agreed between all nine Governments of the NWS, because if they reach agreement on disarmament, it will be a short step to bring the NNWS in the NPT on board, too. The answer is to trust and verify.

Trust and verify

Extend the hand of trust and build a solution to make disarmament work based on a verification process where all parties, including the NWS, need to comply with verification. In other words, generate a proverbial "level playing ground" between the parties.

Such a trust building process needs to involve those people who understand the process of trust building and transformation; that is essential. It is very likely that when all the parties come together to agree to nuclear disarmament they will then also be much more willing to go down the road of discussing general disarmament, which is also an aim embodied in the NPT and the UN Charter. In fact this could easily all happen at the same time. For example, Russia has been observed to be worried about giving up nuclear weapons in case this is just a ruse to leave the US with supreme power in traditional strategic and tactical weapons. This means it is fairly easy, and perhaps inevitable, to link general disarmament to the concept of nuclear disarmament.

Is this all possible?

Possible? Of course it is. Can we do it? In the words of President Obama in his Prague speech, "yes we can". Service and renewal contracts might be in place, but they can be ended: governments have that ability, which they often use.

The author's goal for 2015 is that the April NPT review conference sets in train a process of discussion between all of the NWS parties, preferably by bringing them within the Treaty in some manner or another, and that on September 26, 2015 they will be able to begin to agree to a documented verified nuclear disarmament process to be complete by 2020; then, that this process can be confirmed by the UN General Assembly in 2015. The 26th of September is International Day for the Total Elimination of Nuclear Weapons, which the UN Secretary General, Ban Ki-Moon, designated in 2014, in an effort to move this agenda on.

A greater vision

There is a greater vision where the world can develop by focusing on the factors that build trust and interconnection rather than on the factors that build suspicion and division. The world will then be free to be able to work to the future alignment of nations, each working to contribute their strength to support humanity and the ecosystem in the very same way that citizens, cities, countries and states within nations already work to support their nation, at least in the majority of the world. The nations need to come together to make this happen. This is the spirit of the founding of the United Nations.

The paradigm shift is already occurring; it has been happening for the last 70 years. We can see what it is, a movement for the world to trust more. The author trusts that this will happen.

Right now is the right time, because of the interconnection of minds around the world brought about by the internet, and because of the spirit of collaboration and cooperation that this brings.

Transforming Global Security

Right now is the right time for concerted action, in an important sequence of 25-year events:

1945 - The United Nations was established and called for disarmament.

1970 – The NPT came into force for 25 years.

1995 – The NPT was extended indefinitely.

2020 – Disarmament (the elimination of nuclear weapons) is expected.

It is worth reminding the world that the Mayors for Peace programme, started in 2003, by the Mayors of Nagasaki and Hiroshima, was to see the elimination of nuclear weapons by the year 2020. That was their 2020 vision programme.

By a strange coincidence, the author had also set up a company called 2020 Vision Limited some nine years previously, in 1994, for the 50th anniversary of the UN in 1995, to look at how to run the world by the year 2020. All of these visions could come together by the year 2020 to confirm complete and verified nuclear disarmament by 2020. It could even be possible to achieve general disarmament, not just nuclear disarmament, by 2025, and with it the end of war as an acceptable mechanism for resolving differences of opinion.

If President Kennedy could get a man on the moon in eight years – and not even be alive to see it achieved – the world can get to nuclear disarmament in five years from 2015 to 2020.

That is the mission for the NPT over the next five years:

Glass's Goal: "To achieve *at least* complete and verified global nuclear disarmament by 2020", with the ultimate goal being, by 2025, to end war as a way of resolving differences of opinion.

Further reading

The author believes that these books are absolutely key reading for anybody in the field of disarmament because they contain important information which provides the foundation for changing beliefs and moving into the transformed resolution of the problem – the next paradigm shift.

"The President's Legacy: the world is waiting..." by Gordan Glass; Publ. by www.GlobalLeadershipLtd.com, 2014; ISBN 978-1-910268-00-1

"Eliminating Nuclear Threats", The report of the International Commission on Nuclear Non-proliferation and Disarmament, co-chaired by Gareth Evans and Yoriko Kawaguchi; Publ. by www.ICNND.org, 2009; ISBN 978-1-921612-14-5

"Security without Nuclear Deterrence" by Commander Robert Green; Publ. by www.AstronMedia.com & www.disarmsecure.org, 2010; ISBN 978-0-473-16781-3

"The Speed of Trust" by Stephen M. R. Covey; Publ. by Simon & Schuster, 2006; ISBN 978-0-743295-60-4

During production of this report, the following book came to the author's attention. It describes the transformation process and gives examples:

"The 3rd Alternative" by Stephen R. Covey; Publ. by Simon & Schuster, 2011; ISBN 978-0-85720-513-1

See: www.reinventors.net:

Reinvent Nuclear Security;

An Alternative Future for the National Labs (3 Feb 2015)